Be the Best

SOFTBALL

A Step-By-Step Guide

FOREWORD

by Judi Garman

I grew up on the prairies of western Canada. That's where I learned the game of softball. I had a bat and a pancake of a glove. I also had a wonderful mother who taught me to play. My first softball game was at a Sunday school picnic. Dreams of being a superstar filled my head. Little did I know then of the doors softball would open for me.

I've played on and coached national championship softball teams. I've been on the staff of a team that won the gold medal at the Pan American games. And I have a full-time job coaching softball at a major university. Through a bat and a ball, dreams do come true!

Whatever your dreams or goals may be, softball is a sport you'll love to play. And this book will help you do that. Read it carefully and follow the tips for play. A wonderful world awaits you.

Judi Garman

Judi Garman is among the most successful college softball coaches ever. From 1975 to 1978, she coached Golden West College in California to four straight national junior-college titles. Since 1980, Judi has been the head coach of the women's softball team at California State University, Fullerton. Her winning percentage there is well over 75 percent, and in 1986 the team won the NCAA Division One championship. Judi was elected president of the National Softball Coaches Association in 1988.

Contents

Chapter	Title	Page
1	Softball Is a Fun Sport	7
2	The Story of Softball	8
3	The Game of Softball	12
4	Throwing and Catching a Softball	23
5	Slow-Pitch Pitching	28
6	Fast-Pitch Pitching	31
7	Fielding	37
8	Hitting	50
9	Base Running	58
10	Sportsmanship	63

Softball Is a Fun Sport

Softball is a game that's fun for everyone. It is played by young and old alike.

What makes softball so popular? It is probably because there are two different kinds of softball: slow-pitch and fast-pitch. In slow-pitch softball, every batter has a chance to be a star hitter because pitchers are not allowed to throw fast. The emphasis is on hitting the ball in slow-pitch softball. Fast-pitch softball, however, is harder and appeals to those who like tougher competition. The pitchers are allowed to throw the ball as fast as they want.

Whether slow-pitch or fast-pitch, softball offers something for nearly everyone. And this book will help you get the most out of playing the game.

The Story of Softball

The game of softball is almost as old as the game of baseball. The first softball game was played at the Farragut Boat Club in Chicago in November 1887. The inventor of softball was a member of the boat club named George Hancock.

One afternoon, Hancock was stuck inside the club's gymnasium because of bad weather. He was bored and wanted something to do. Hancock tied up an old boxing glove to look like a ball. That padded glove became the very first softball. He then cut off a broomstick to use as a bat.

"Let's play an indoor ball game," he called to his friends. Teams were picked and bases marked off. On

that stormy November day, Hancock and his pals played the very first softball game indoors at a boat club on Lake Michigan.

Hancock so enjoyed the new ball game that he decided to write up a set of rules for it. George Hancock not only wrote softball's first official rules, but he also went on to develop the first real softball and rubber-tipped softball bat.

During the months that followed, Hancock and his friends continued to play their new indoor version of baseball. Eventually, softball caught on and spread. For a time, the game was called by such names as "indoor baseball" and "pumpkin ball."

In 1900, the game of softball was finally moved outdoors. Firefighting companies in Minneapolis, Minnesota, began to play an outdoor version of Hancock's game called kitten ball. Kitten ball's great popularity gave birth to the very first softball league, established in Minneapolis in 1900. The league published the first complete set of softball rules and regulations.

In the 1920s, softball was called mush ball, big ball, or diamond ball. The game was becoming very popular. But the rules still differed from place to place. In 1926, an attempt was made to come up with standard rules. The National Recreation Congress met to set down a list of regulations, but the meeting was unsuccessful. At that meeting, however, Walter Hakanson of the Denver YMCA was the first person officially to call the game softball.

Softball's popularity soared in the late 1920s and in the early 1930s. In 1933, a sportswriter named Leo Fischer helped organize the National Softball Tournament. It was played at Chicago's Exposition of Progress, similar to a modern world's fair. The big tournament was extremely successful. Afterward, the game's first *uniform* rules were drawn up. The game was officially named softball.

To enforce the rules and govern the game, the American Softball Association was formed. Its first president was Leo Fischer.

Through the work of the ASA, softball has grown into one of America's favorite pastimes. Every year, the ASA sponsors national softball tournaments crowning champions in many divisions, both amateur and professional.

The Game of Softball

Softball is much like the game of baseball. The major differences between softball and baseball are the size of the ball, how the ball is pitched to the batter, and the size of the playing field.

A softball is about twice the size of a baseball. It is also a bit softer. But you still should use a glove to catch a softball.

Baseball pitchers throw overhand to the batter. A softball pitcher *must* throw underhand to the batter. There are different pitching rules for slow-pitch and fast-pitch games. In general, a slow-pitch hurler allows the batter to hit the ball and relies on his or her defensive teammates to get the batters out. A fast-pitch hurler throws hard and tries to strike out batters.

PITCHERS THROW UNDERHAND IN SOFTBALL

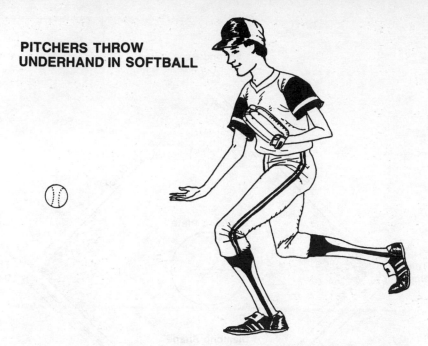

A softball does not travel as far or as fast as a baseball. This is why a softball field is usually smaller than a baseball field. The distance from the pitcher's mound to home base is shorter in softball than in baseball, as are the distances between the bases.

A slow-pitch softball team is made up of ten players. That is one more than a regulation fast-pitch team, which has nine players. However, any number of players can play on a side for a friendly game.

What do you need to play a friendly game of softball? That is an easy question to answer. All you need are a softball, a bat, a glove, a small level field, some friends, and bases.

First, you have to arrange the bases in a diamond shape. Homemade bases can be squares of cardboard or even paper. Start by placing home base so that it faces out to the biggest part of the field. Next, stand on home

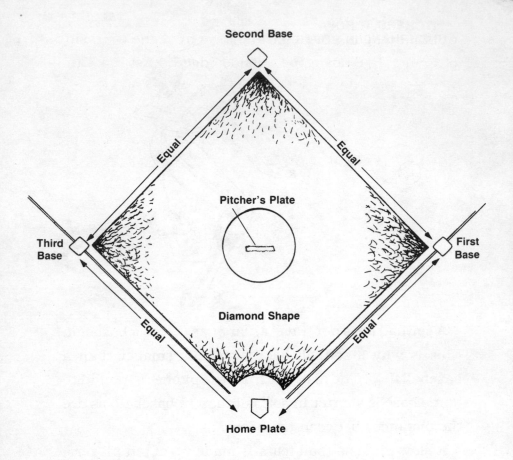

Second Base

Equal

Equal

Pitcher's Plate

Third
Base

First
Base

Diamond Shape

Equal

Equal

Home Plate

base and face toward the open part of the field. Place the bases in a diamond shape so first base is to your right, second base is straight out from home, and third base is to your left. The bases should measure an equal distance apart.

The pitcher's mound, or the place where the pitcher will throw from, is usually a few feet less than half-way between home base and second base.

Home base is where the ball is batted from. A player stands beside home, never on it, and attempts to hit a pitched ball into the fair field of play.

Fair territory is any part of the field inside imaginary or real straight lines. One line runs from the right side of home plate down the outside edge of first base and into the outfield. On the other side, the line runs from the left side of home plate down the outside edge of third base and out into the outfield. Balls hit outside of fair territory are *foul balls* and do not count.

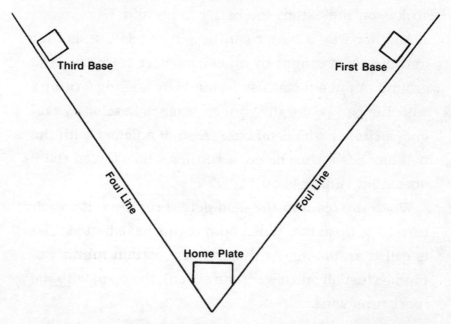

When a ball is batted into fair territory, the batter becomes a runner. The runner must advance from base to base, moving from home plate to first base, to second base, to third base, and then to home plate again. Anytime a runner goes around the bases and touches home safely, a point called a *run* is scored. The object of a softball game is to score more runs than the other team. During play, a runner can stop at any base but must wait for the next opportunity to advance.

The goal of the players in the field is to get the team up at bat out as quickly as possible, with few or no runs scored. A batter can be *put out* by swinging at three pitched balls and missing them. A swing and a miss at a pitched ball is called a *strike*. Three strikes and a batter is out. Balls hit into foul territory count as strikes except for a third strike. If a ball is hit foul with two strikes on the batter, the batter is not out.

Another way a batter can be put out is if a ball hit into the air is caught by a fielder before it touches the ground. A put out can also be made by tagging a runner with the ball before the runner reaches base or by tagging a runner who is off base. Also, if a fielder with the ball touches a base before a runner who's forced there does, that runner is out.

When the team in the field gets three outs, it's their turn to be up at bat. When both teams have batted, that is called an *inning*. At the end of a certain number of innings (usually no fewer than seven), the team with the most runs wins.

REGULATION PLAY

An official regulation softball game is made up of seven innings. An umpire calls balls and strikes in both slow-pitch and fast-pitch games. To be a *called strike* (one not swung at) in slow-pitch softball, the ball must be pitched over home plate no lower than the top of the batter's knees and no higher than the batter's highest shoulder. For fast-pitch softball, the *strike zone* is the top of the batter's knees and the batter's armpits.

THE STRIKE ZONE

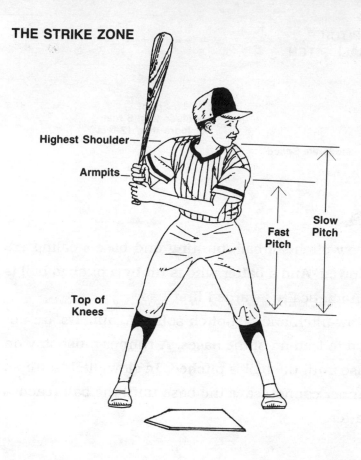

Highest Shoulder—

Armpits—

Slow Pitch

Fast Pitch

Top of Knees

Pitches swung at and missed also count as strikes. Pitches that are not in the strike zone and not swung at are called *balls.* After four balls are pitched, the batter gets to go to first base free. This is called a *walk.*

For slow-pitch games, there are other special rules. A slow-pitched ball must travel at moderate speed and have an arc at least six feet but not higher than twelve feet above the ground. (An "arc" means the ball must go up and then down, forming a curve when viewed from the side.) A pitcher who throws fast in slow-pitch softball can be thrown out of the game.

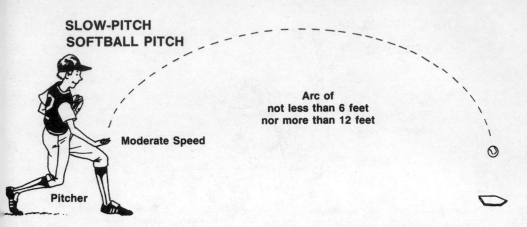

SLOW-PITCH SOFTBALL PITCH

Arc of
not less than 6 feet
nor more than 12 feet

Moderate Speed

Pitcher

In slow-pitch softball, bunting and base stealing are not allowed. And a batter who is hit by a pitched ball is not automatically awarded first base.

In slow-pitch and fast-pitch softball, runners are not allowed to lead off of the bases. A runner must stay on the base until the ball is pitched. In slow-pitch softball, the runner cannot leave the base until the ball reaches the batter.

THE FIELD

The size of a regulation softball field can vary according to the age of the players and the type of game (slow-pitch or fast-pitch).

For players aged ten or younger, the distance between bases on a softball field should be fifty-five feet. For players eleven to twelve years old, the distance between bases should be sixty feet. Fast-pitch softball players older than that also play on a field with bases sixty feet apart. Slow-pitch softball players aged thirteen or older play on a field with bases sixty-five feet apart.

FIELD FOR PLAYERS 9-12

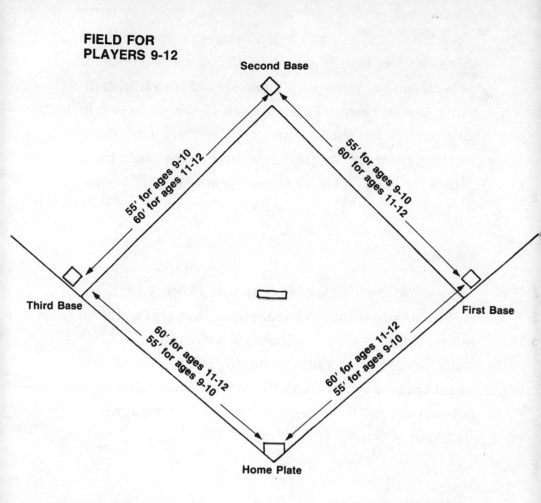

Second Base

55' for ages 9-10
60' for ages 11-12

55' for ages 9-10
60' for ages 11-12

Third Base

First Base

60' for ages 11-12
55' for ages 9-10

60' for ages 11-12
55' for ages 9-10

Home Plate

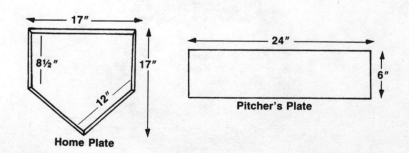

17"

8½"

17"

12"

Home Plate

24"

6"

Pitcher's Plate

Softball pitchers aged ten or younger should stand thirty-five feet from home plate. In fast-pitch games for girls eleven or twelve, a pitcher should also hurl from thirty-five feet away. Pitchers aged eleven or twelve in slow-pitch games should stand forty feet from home plate. That forty-foot pitching distance also applies to fast-pitch games for boys eleven or twelve years old.

THE BALL

A modern softball is not really soft. However, it is not as hard as a baseball. There are many kinds of softballs, but not all of them are allowed in official play.

For junior play (ages nine to twelve), a softball measures between 11⅞ and 12⅛ inches around. It weighs between 6¼ and 7 ounces. It is generally called a twelve-inch ball.

INSIDE OF SOFTBALL

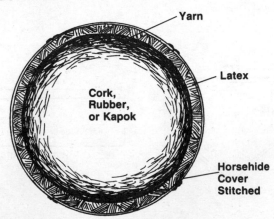

Yarn

Latex

Cork,
Rubber,
or Kapok

Horsehide
Cover
Stitched

A softball must be smooth seamed or flat surfaced. It is filled with cork or rubber, and sometimes it's a mixture of both. Occasionally, a sticky fiber called kapok (mattress padding) is used. Next, yarn is wound around the inside filling. It is then coated with latex (a rubbery substance) or rubber cement. Over that goes a cover of horsehide.

Some softballs have seams with thick stitches; others do not.

BATS

Almost all softball bats today are made of aluminum. However, a softball bat can be made of wood, nylon, or magnesium. Bats come in a variety of lengths and types.

CATCHING EQUIPMENT

Slow-pitch catchers wear a helmet and a light catcher's mask with thick padding. The rules state that girls must also wear chest protectors when catching for slow-pitch games. Catchers for fast-pitch games wear full catching gear, which includes a mask, a helmet, a chest protector, and usually hard plastic shin guards.

GLOVES

In softball, the rules make a distinction between a glove and a mitt. A glove has a separate finger space for each finger. A mitt does not have a separate space for

FIRST-BASE MITT   **FIELDER'S GLOVE**

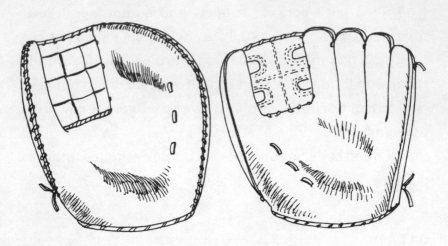

each finger. A mitt has a space for the thumb only. The rest of the hand fits in the other space. Only catchers and first basemen are allowed to wear mitts.

In general, softball gloves are bigger than baseball gloves. Softball gloves have deep pockets and wide webbing.

SHOES

Sneakers are fine for playing softball. Baseball-type metal cleats are not allowed for young players. The spiked shoes that are allowed for young softball players have rounded, molded cleats made of plastic or hard rubber. They provide good traction and are safe.

Throwing and Catching a Softball

Basic softball skills center on throwing and catching the ball well. What follows is an explanation of how those skills can be acquired and sharpened.

GRIP

The grip is how you hold the ball before you throw it. The size of your hand may determine your grip. The most common way to grip the ball is the *four-finger grip*. The ball is held firmly by the thumb at the bottom and the first three fingers on the top. Your little finger is on the side of the ball to steady it in your hand.

FOUR-FINGER SOFTBALL
THROWING GRIP

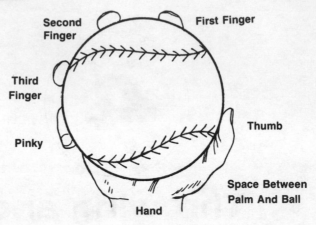

If your hand is larger, your fingers will automatically stretch farther and give you more control of the ball. Putting your fingers across the seams will also help keep the ball from slipping out of your grip.

The *full-finger grip* is another way to hold the ball. It is a good way to hold the ball if your hands are small. In the full-finger grip, all five fingers are around the ball. Your middle finger should be on top. Your thumb and

FULL-FINGER
THROWING GRIP

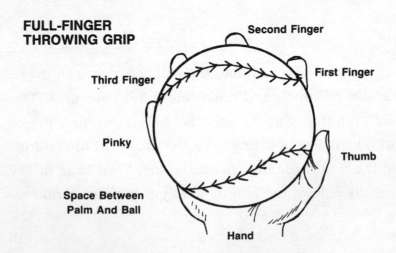

pinky should be on the bottom. Make sure the ball rests just on your fingertips and not against the palm, or flat, of your hand. Otherwise, your throw will be inaccurate.

STEP AND THROW

Grip the ball and cock or bend your arm to throw it. Remember, *only* the pitcher throws underhand in softball. Fielders use an overhand throw. Shift your weight to your back foot, which is the foot on the side you throw with. (For example, it would be your right foot if you're right-handed.) With your arm cocked back behind your body, step toward your target with the foot opposite your throwing arm. Point your glove at your target. As you step, bring your arm forward and whip the ball.

As you step and throw, the weight of your body shifts forward. That is called *getting your body into the throw.* As your hand comes forward and points at the target, release the ball with a snap of your wrist. Once you release the ball, do not stop your arm and body from continuing forward on their downward motion. Allow your arm and weight to go forward. Your weight is now completely shifted to your front leg. That is called a *follow-through.*

Just as in grips, there are several different kinds of throws. There is the *sidearm* throw, which is good for short, quick throws in the infield. However, the sidearm throw is not always that accurate.

There is also the *basic overhand* throw, which is the throw beginners should use. It is accurate and powerful.

The ball starts behind the body and comes over the top of the shoulder just above the ear. Your elbow should stay shoulder high or higher.

Finally, there is the *three-quarter throw*. It is a motion halfway between the sidearm toss and an overhand throw. It is a throw many athletes use.

THREE KINDS OF THROWS

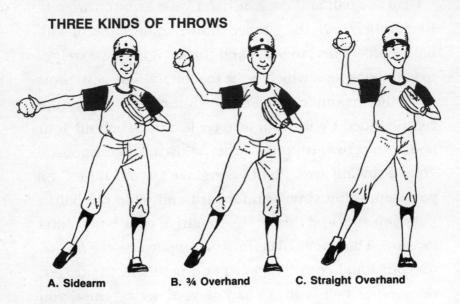

A. Sidearm   B. ¾ Overhand   C. Straight Overhand

WARMING UP

Warming up is a way to get your arm ready to throw hard during a game. Never throw hard to start. Always throw easy at first to get your muscles ready to work harder. Using proper mechanics, throw easy for five or ten minutes before throwing hard.

CATCHING A SOFTBALL

To catch a softball thrown to you, keep your eyes on it at all times. Don't turn your head away. Try to get your body in front of the ball so you won't have to reach

CATCHING

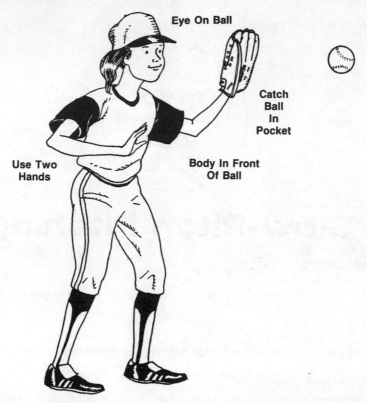

Eye On Ball

Catch Ball In Pocket

Use Two Hands

Body In Front Of Ball

out to the side for it. You want the ball to hit your glove in the *pocket*. That's the webbing strung between the thumb and first finger.

Do not put your index finger in the first finger of the glove—double two fingers together. That will give you a bigger pocket overall. Glove fingertips should point up for throws coming in above the waist, and down for throws coming in below the waist. Use two hands for catching.

Put your free hand behind your glove at the thumb and webbing. The free hand will help close the glove around a ball and help make a quick release.

Slow-Pitch Pitching

In slow-pitch softball, the pitcher's delivery is much like tossing a horseshoe or rolling a bowling ball.

To start, stand on the pitcher's plate (see page 14) and face the batter. Do not be tense or stand rigid. For the most part, you will use a four-finger grip (see page 23). Hold the ball in front of you with two hands.

The rules for a slow-pitch game require the pitcher to touch the pitcher's plate with at least one foot before the wind-up. This will be the foot you will use to push off of when you pitch. If you are a right-handed pitcher, keep your right foot on the pitcher's plate. (Reverse if left-handed.)

To make the pitch legal, the start position must be held for at least one second before you pitch. Then you can begin your pitching motion by stepping back

SLOW-PITCH PITCHING

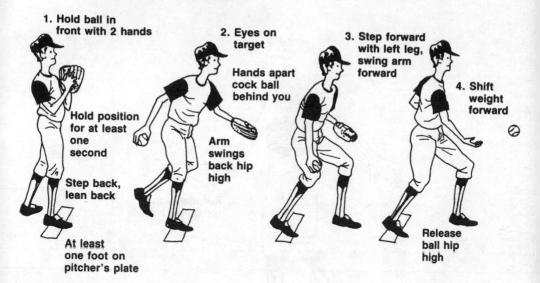

1. Hold ball in front with 2 hands

Hold position for at least one second

Step back, lean back

At least one foot on pitcher's plate

2. Eyes on target

Hands apart cock ball behind you

Arm swings back hip high

3. Step forward with left leg, swing arm forward

4. Shift weight forward

Release ball hip high

behind the pitcher's plate with your left foot (your right foot if left-handed) or stepping directly forward. Your pivot foot (the one you'll push off with) must stay in contact with the pitcher's plate until the ball is released.

Pull your hands apart and cock the ball behind your body as your right arm swings back. (Reverse if left-handed.) The rules state that your arm swing cannot go higher than your hip on the back swing or the front swing when you bring your arm forward to release the ball.

Step forward with your left leg (your right leg if left-handed), and swing your arm forward underhanded at the same time. Keep your eyes on the target—the catcher's glove. Remember that the ball must be thrown in an arc at least six feet above where the ball is released but not higher than twelve feet above the ground. It

LEGAL ARM SWING

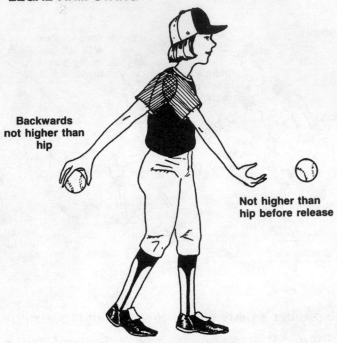

Backwards not higher than hip

Not higher than hip before release

must be of moderate speed. Arcing the ball helps it come toward the batter slowly.

A number of young softball pitchers feel awkward when taking that first step back to pitch. If you feel that way, go into your arm motion and step forward directly. Do not step back. Just remember to pause a second at the start. You also must keep your pivot foot in contact with the pitcher's plate until you release the ball.

After releasing the ball, step or jump back and be prepared. Because slow-pitch softball is a hitter's game, the ball might be slammed back at you.

In a slow-pitch game, there are no trick pitches to use. To pitch well, you must have control and throw strikes.

Fast-Pitch Pitching

Fast-pitch softball is a duel between the pitcher and the batter. And because the distance from the pitcher's plate to home base is so close (35 or 40 feet), a pitcher with good control and speed has the advantage.

Wait for the batter to get into a ready-to-hit stance. Then stand with one foot on the pitcher's plate and your other foot on or behind the rubber as in slow pitching. Face the batter, keeping your hands apart. The ball can be in your glove or in your pitching hand.

The catcher will now give you the signal for what pitch to throw. After getting the signal, hold the ball in both hands for not less than one second and not more than ten seconds. Then pitch.

There are several different kinds of pitches to use in fast-pitch softball. Different grips, pressure points, and releases make the ball spin in the air. And different spins make the ball move differently.

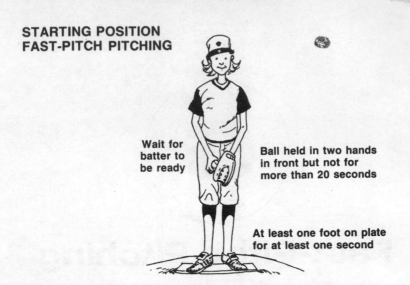

**STARTING POSITION
FAST-PITCH PITCHING**

Wait for
batter to
be ready

Ball held in two hands
in front but not for
more than 20 seconds

At least one foot on plate
for at least one second

WINDMILL AND SLINGSHOT

In fast-pitch softball, there are several kinds of deliveries or ways to get the ball to the plate. The best two are the *windmill* and the *slingshot*.

For the windmill delivery as a right-handed pitcher, your weight should be on your right foot. Hide your grip from the batter by keeping the hand with the ball behind your glove. Keeping both hands together, stretch your arms down so they are comfortably extended. With your front foot, start to step toward the batter. Lift the hand with the ball out of your glove and over your head, making a big circle in the air. Your arm should brush past your ear. As the ball reaches the highest point over your head, your left foot should be firmly on the ground and your hips should be perpendicular to the batter. (Reverse if left-handed.)

The ball and your arm should now start downward in the delivery motion. It is a windmill-like movement up over your head, which is how this delivery got its name. You may only wind your arm around in this fashion one time for a pitch to be legal. Spinning your arm around and around would be illegal.

As your right arm completes its windmill cycle and comes forward, release the ball at hip level. At the same time, shift your weight forward to the left foot and push off with the right foot. (Reverse if left-handed.)

Because of this arm motion, the windmill delivery propels the ball at great speed.

FAST-PITCH WINDMILL DELIVERY

1. Start position

2. Arm drawn back up over head

3. Left foot steps toward batter

4. Arm goes downward

5.

6. Ball released at hips as weight shifts forward

Side view of windmill delivery

SLINGSHOT DELIVERY

1.
Turn body to side as you stride

2.
Step and whip arm releasing with sharp wrist snap

Ball drawn way behind back

The slingshot delivery is not as fast but may be easier to learn than the windmill delivery. It is more of a simple backward cocking of the arm and then a snap motion forward. The wind-up starts like the windmill wind-up, except your hands are near the right side of your body. (Reverse if left-handed.) After separating your hands, draw the ball way back behind your body in a circular motion with the ball and your palm facing the ground. As the ball is drawn back, turn sideways. Your arm should reach as high as possible. Shift your weight to your left foot. Then come down and forward with your throwing arm, releasing it with a sharp wrist snap at your right hip, and push hard with your right foot.

DROP-PITCH GRIP

To throw a drop pitch, grip the ball across the seams with your thumb and first three fingers. Your other finger should be on the side of the ball. When your hand comes forward, release your thumb first. Follow through with your palm up and let your arm come up over your head. This will make the ball roll off your first three fingers. It will also make the ball spin counterclockwise, causing it to sink as it approaches the batter.

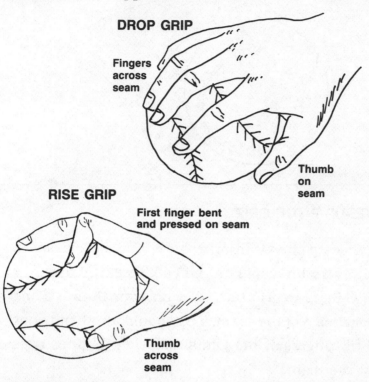

DROP GRIP

Fingers across seam

Thumb on seam

RISE GRIP

First finger bent and pressed on seam

Thumb across seam

RISE-PITCH GRIP

Several grips will cause a pitched ball to rise. But one of the best ways to throw a rise pitch is to hold the ball by your thumb and first two fingers. Bend your first finger at the joint, pressing the fingertip on the ball at the seam. This grip will give the ball a reverse or back spin, making it rise when it's pitched. The release is like turning a doorknob to the right. The ball rolls over the inside of the middle finger.

CHANGE-UP GRIP

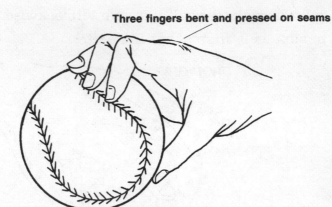

Three fingers bent and pressed on seams

CHANGE-UP PITCH GRIP

A change-up pitch is thrown slower than normal speed and with very little spin on the ball. One way to throw a change-up is to grip the ball with your thumb along the widest part of the seam. You should also bend your first three fingers at the joints, pressing the fingertips against the seam.

For an easier change-up pitch use your normal grip but hold the ball deep in your hand so you are palming the ball. Hold tightly with your thumb and little finger. Your other fingers should be placed loosely on the ball. At the release, push the ball toward the batter.

Fielding

In softball, especially in a slow-pitch game, fielding is extremely important. A pitcher cannot strike out every batter. The fielders must help the pitcher get the batter out.

READY POSITION

If you stand straight up, you will not be able to get to the ball quickly or field it smoothly. To get in a good ready position, spread your feet about shoulder width or a bit wider. Bend forward at the waist and place your hands *lightly* on your knees. Knees are slightly bent. *Do not* rest on your knees by placing all of your weight on your hands. Your weight should be on the balls of your feet, not on your heels. Maintain a good balanced position. Now you are ready to field.

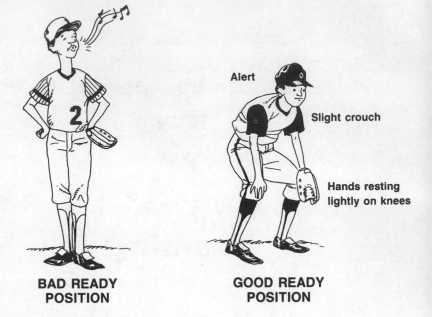

BAD READY POSITION

GOOD READY POSITION

Alert

Slight crouch

Hands resting lightly on knees

FIELDING GROUND BALLS

To field a ground ball, you must position yourself correctly. Quickly move into a position where you can field the ball in the middle of your body. That's called *getting in front of the ball*. Wherever and whenever you can, get in front of the ball to field it. That way, even if you miss the ball with your glove, you may still be able to stop it with your body.

Go for the ball by bending at the knees. *Do not* keep your knees straight and just bend at the waist. Lower your seat toward the ground by bending those knees. As you crouch to field the ball, keep your eyes on the ball and your weight forward.

Stretch your arms out in front of you, holding your glove open and close to the ground. Field the ball out in front of your body between your legs. And keep that glove low until the ball is actually in it. Otherwise, the ball may scoot under your glove and through your legs.

Use two hands in fielding a ground ball. Once it's in your glove, cover it with your bare hand. Fielding with two hands also saves time in throwing to a base because your throwing hand is already on the ball. It does not have to reach into the glove when you stand up to throw.

If a ball is hit slowly, do not wait for it to come to you. You should move quickly to the ball. That is called *charging the ball*. If need be, you can use just your glove hand to field a slow hit ball. Just remember that two hands are better than one in fielding most ground balls.

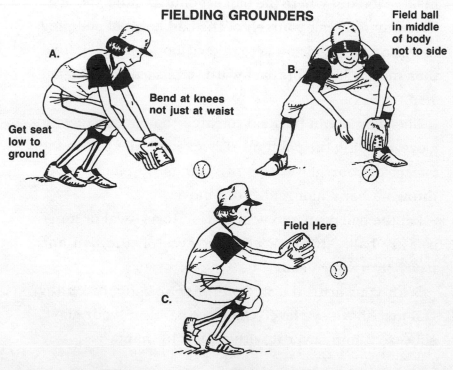

FIELDING GROUNDERS

A.

B.

C.

Field ball in middle of body not to side

Bend at knees not just at waist

Get seat low to ground

Field Here

FIELDING FLY BALLS

To field a fly ball, a player must get into position to catch the ball before it comes down. That is called *getting under the ball*. Run to the spot, then stop and wait for the ball to come down. Do not loaf or run lazily to the spot so that you end up catching the ball on the run.

To get to the spot before the ball does, you must get a "jump on the ball." This means moving in the direction the ball is hit the instant it is hit. It takes practice to do that. But getting a good jump is a big plus for any fielder.

When a ball is hit in the air, do not automatically start moving forward. That is a mistake many beginners make. Find out where the ball is going and then go after it. A way to break yourself of the bad habit of stepping in when a fly ball is hit is to take a short step back first, then move. This short backward step is called a *stagger step*.

Once you are in position to catch the ball, raise your glove, keeping the palm up. Try to catch the ball in the pocket of your glove. *Use two hands* by placing your throwing hand alongside your glove.

Let the ball drop into your glove. Never swat or lunge at a fly ball. Always keep your eyes on the ball and never turn your head.

With your arms out in front of your body, catch the ball just above eye level. Once the ball is in your glove, squeeze it and cover it with your bare hand.

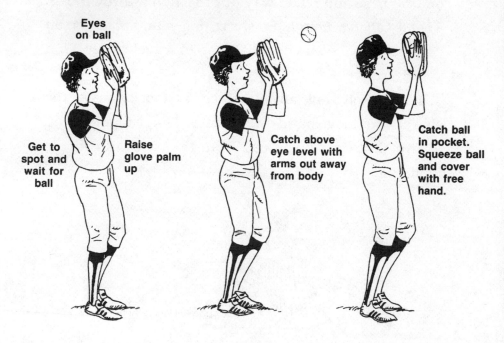

Eyes on ball

Get to spot and wait for ball

Raise glove palm up

Catch above eye level with arms out away from body

Catch ball in pocket. Squeeze ball and cover with free hand.

Once you get better at catching fly balls, start positioning yourself for a throw afterward. Do that by getting under the ball and taking a step back. Then, as you make the catch, take a step forward. That gets your body moving in the direction you will throw, and it also helps get your body into the throw more quickly.

PLAYING FIRST BASE

To play first base, you must be able to catch the ball well. A first-base person needs agility and quick reactions. On most teams, the first-base person is tall and lanky with long arms and legs. It is not necessary to be built like that, but it helps in getting out runners.

A tall person with long arms and legs can put one foot on first base and reach way out to catch a thrown ball. That is called a *stretch*. By stretching, a first-base person cuts down the distance a ball has to travel to get out a speedy runner.

When stretching, always place the foot *opposite* the side of your glove hand on the base. That will allow you to stretch as far as you can from the base your foot is touching.

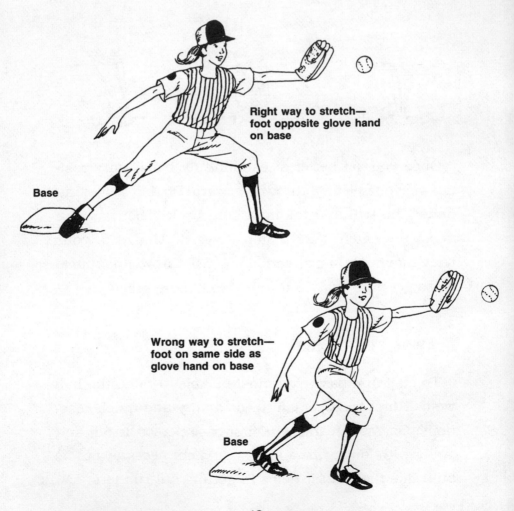

Right way to stretch—foot opposite glove hand on base

Base

Wrong way to stretch—foot on same side as glove hand on base

Base

When playing first base, do not stand right on it. Stand in the infield to the side of the base and several steps in front of it. When a ball is hit, go to the base and position yourself to receive the throw. To do that, stand by the edge of the base nearest fair territory, with your glove up and facing the fielder who will throw to you. Place the foot opposite the side of your glove hand on the edge of first base. Never put your foot on the middle of the base. Otherwise, the runner may step on your foot and injure it.

TAKING A THROW AT FIRST
CORRECT POSITION

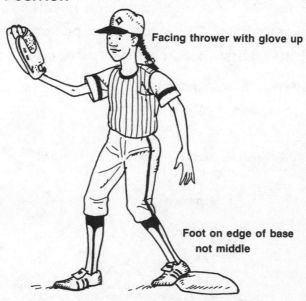

Facing thrower with glove up

Foot on edge of base
not middle

Your first job is to catch every ball possible. That means taking your foot off the base if you have to. If you miss the ball, the runner will go to second. If you catch it but take your foot off first base, the runner will be safe there.

PLAYING SECOND BASE AND SHORTSTOP

The second-base person and the shortstop are the two best ground-ball fielders on the team. Both players have to be alert and quick. They must also have good hands. The shortstop plays halfway between second and third base. The second-base person plays halfway between second and first base.

The shortstop and second-base person must work well together to make *double plays*. A double play can take place when a runner is on first base. A batter hits the ball to the shortstop. The shortstop throws the ball to second. The second-base person tags the base to force out one runner. The second-base person then turns and throws to first base to get the batter out. A double play

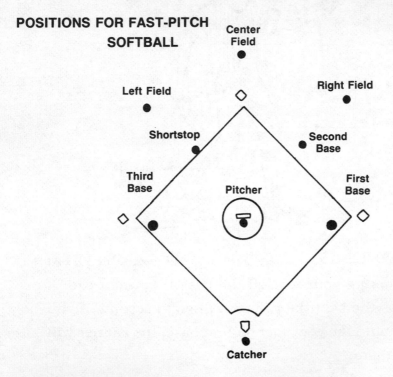

POSITIONS FOR FAST-PITCH SOFTBALL

Center Field

Left Field

Right Field

Shortstop

Second Base

Third Base

Pitcher

First Base

Catcher

must be done smoothly and quickly to get both the runner and the batter out.

Sometimes a double play will work in reverse, with the second-base person throwing to the shortstop who covers second base and then throws to first. Other infielders can also start a double play. The shortstop and second-base person each will cover second base in different situations.

Because the base paths are so short in softball, double plays are very hard to make. However, a good softball rule is always to get the lead runner (the one going to second base) out and don't worry so much about the hitter. Once you get the lead runner out, making a double play becomes a bonus.

POSITIONS FOR SLOW-PITCH SOFTBALL

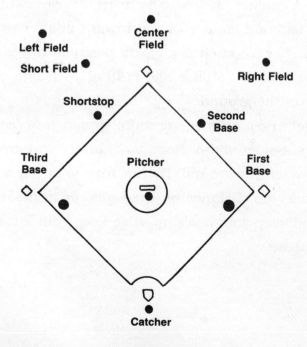

PLAYING THIRD BASE

Third base is sometimes called the *hot corner*. That is because a lot of sharply hit balls go to third. To play third base, you must be alert, have quick reflexes, and make strong and accurate throws.

A third-base person must also be good at charging balls that are bunted or hit slowly. The third-base person does not play on the base. Like the first-base person, he or she stands in the ready position to the inside of the base and in front of it.

PLAYING CATCHER

The catcher is like an army general. He or she is in charge of the infield. A catcher has to have stamina and strong legs. Crouching to receive pitches can be very tiring. A catcher must also be nearly fearless—unafraid of the ball or a runner racing toward home base.

A catcher's crouch is a ready position, *not* a resting position. Never catch while resting with one or both knees on the ground.

To get into a catcher's crouch, spread your feet apart about shoulder width. Bend your knees and drop your seat toward the ground. Do not turn your heels too far in under you. Balance on the balls, or fronts, of your feet and keep your heels up. Also keep your knees open and spread.

CATCHER'S CROUCH

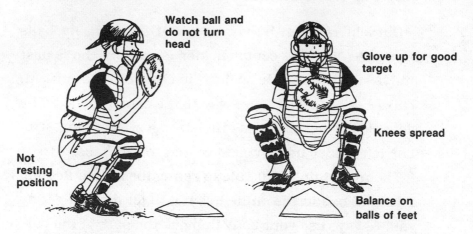

Watch ball and do not turn head

Glove up for good target

Knees spread

Not resting position

Balance on balls of feet

When catching, give the pitcher a good target. Hold your glove up for the pitcher to look at, and keep it in that spot until the pitch. It's usually a good idea to move the target to a different area around the plate for each pitch. Put your bare hand behind your glove so your fingers don't get hit with foul balls.

Catchers must try to *block* any balls that can't be caught. To block a ball, drop down on both knees in the direct path of the ball. Hold your glove low with your fingers pointing toward the ground. Tuck your chin in so you can see the ball.

PLAYING THE OUTFIELD

Outfielders must be very good at catching fly balls (see page 40). The center fielder is usually the fastest and best outfielder. He or she is in charge of the outfield. The other outfielders give way to the center fielder. The right fielder normally has the strongest throwing arm. The left fielder usually gets more ground balls.

The most important rule to remember when fielding a ground ball in the outfield is not to let the ball get by you. Always use your body to block the path of the ball. You can even get down on one knee to field a ground ball in the outfield.

OUTFIELDER FIELDING GROUNDER

On one knee to block its path with body.

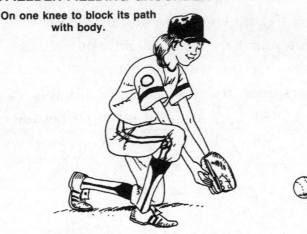

On a ball hit deeply into the outfield, always throw the ball to the cutoff person. The cutoff person is an infielder (second-base person or shortstop) who goes partially into the outfield to reduce the distance the outfielder has to throw the ball. The cutoff person then relays the ball in. Two short throws are faster than one long throw.

**OUTFIELDER MAKING A ONE-
BOUNCE THROW TO A BASE**

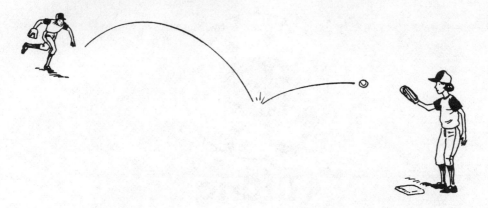

When throwing directly to a base (unless it's just a short distance), throw the ball in on a bounce. The idea is to make the ball bounce once before getting to the base.

PLAYING THE SHORT FIELD

In slow-pitch softball, there are ten players on a team instead of the normal nine. The tenth player plays in shallow left center field or shallow right center field. The short fielder gets a lot of line drives and often cuts off the path of extra-base hits.

Hitting

Hitting, especially in a slow-pitch game, is an important part of softball. Remember, you can't win a game if you don't score runs. Hitting the ball produces runs.

CHOOSING A BAT

Pick a bat that feels comfortable in your hands and is easy to swing. It should not feel heavy or awkward. A coach or parent can help you choose the bat that's right for you. If in doubt, choose the lighter bat.

GRIP

A right-handed batter grips the bat with the left hand closest to the bottom of the bat and the right hand on top of the left hand. (Reverse these hand positions if you bat left-handed.) There should not be any space between your hands. Hold the bat firmly at the base of your fingers (don't palm it) and do not squeeze it too tightly.

Holding the bat at the bottom is called an *end grip* or *long grip*. It gets the leverage of the entire bat into the swing and is a power grip. You can hit the ball far with this grip.

Some hitters use a *choke grip*. A choke grip is when you move your hands higher up the bat and leave a space at the bottom. A choke grip gives you better control of your bat. You will swing and miss less with a choke grip. You can also use a grip somewhere between a choke grip and an end grip.

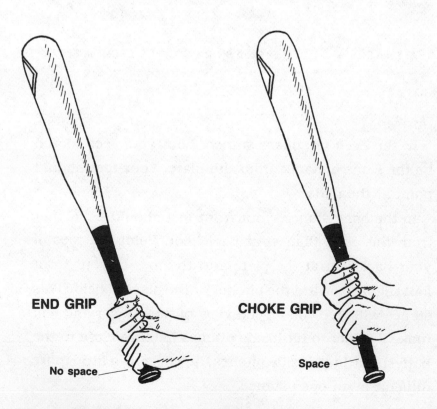

END GRIP

No space

CHOKE GRIP

Space

BATTING STANCE

Your stance is the way you stand to hit a softball. Standing correctly improves your chances of hitting the ball. There are three basic hitting stances. Choose one you feel comfortable with. The three stances are the *even* or *square* stance, the *open* stance, and the *closed* stance. Each differs in how you place your feet alongside the plate.

BATTING STANCES

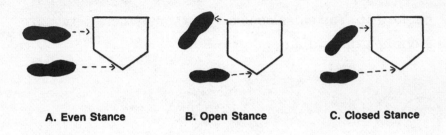

A. Even Stance   **B. Open Stance**   **C. Closed Stance**

In the *even* or *square stance*, both your feet should be the same distance from the plate. Your toes should point *at* the plate.

In the *open stance*, your front foot should be farther from the plate than your back foot. Point the toes of your back foot at the plate and the toes of your front foot slightly toward the pitcher or the playing field. This stance will give you a good view of the pitcher and will make it easier to hit inside pitches (pitches close to the batter). Hitting outside pitches, however, is a little more difficult in an open stance.

In a *closed stance*, your front foot should be closer to the plate than your back foot. This stance will allow you to hit both inside and outside pitches well.

Make sure the stance you choose feels comfortable. Keep your weight evenly balanced and your body relaxed. Hold your arms away from your body, and keep your bat chest high or higher. *Never* hold your bat lower than chest high, and never keep your arms tightly in against your body. Your elbows should be bent at a ninety degree angle.

If it feels comfortable to bend your knees slightly in your stance, then do it. The important thing is good balance!

CONCENTRATION

When you're at home plate and ready to hit, concentrate on the ball at the pitcher's release point. Watch it all the way in. Only swing at pitches in the strike zone (see page 16). Those are the best ones to hit.

TIMING YOUR SWING

Perfect timing is swinging and hitting the ball at precisely the moment you want to. How the ball is hit and where it goes are often an indication of your timing and swing.

A line-drive hit up the middle usually means your timing is perfect and your swing is level. Hitting fly balls means you are swinging up or uppercutting the ball slightly.

Hitting the ball to the opposite field (for example, to right field if you're a right-handed hitter) usually means your timing is late.

Pulling the ball means hitting it to left field if you're right-handed or to right field if you're left-handed. Some batters do this intentionally. But others do it accidentally when they swing too soon, hitting the ball before it reaches home plate.

Hitting ground balls sometimes means you are swinging down instead of level.

It is impossible to time every pitch perfectly. Pulling the ball or swinging a bit late occasionally is okay. That is what makes hitting such a duel between the batter and the pitcher. What a batter always wants to do is hit the ball and put it into play, *not* strike out. (But remember that even the best of hitters strike out sometimes.) A level swing and good timing will reduce the number of times you strike out.

A. Swinging and
hitting ball late

B. Perfect
timing

C. Hitting ball out in
front or pulling ball

HITTING THE BALL

When you go to home plate to bat, measure your distance from the plate with your bat. The fat part of your bat should reach over the entire plate easily. Take some practice swings to relax, then get set in your stance. Concentrate on the pitcher. Never turn your head away or close your eyes as the pitch approaches.

Time your swing as the ball comes toward the plate. Take a short stride forward with your front foot. That is called *stepping into the pitch*. As you start your swing, pivot on your back foot. Your shoulders should remain level to help keep your swing level. Keep your elbows bent until contact. Then extend your arms as you drive the bat into the ball, and *keep your eyes on the ball!*

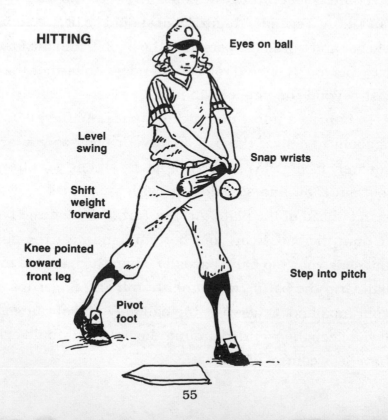

HITTING

Eyes on ball

Level swing

Snap wrists

Shift weight forward

Knee pointed toward front leg

Step into pitch

Pivot foot

Your weight stays balanced. As you finish your swing, use your wrists to whip or snap the bat as you make contact with the ball. Follow through by allowing the bat and your arms to swing around your body.

After hitting the ball, drop the bat to the ground. Never release it during the finish of the swing, and never throw the bat. That is very dangerous.

BUNTING

Bunting is not allowed in slow-pitch softball. But it is allowed in fast-pitch softball. Knowing how to bunt can help win a fast-pitch softball game, especially against a really good pitcher.

A bunt is just hitting the ball softly with the bat without taking a swing. A bunted ball should go between the pitcher and third-base person or the pitcher and the first-base person. It should roll softly and go no farther than just beyond the pitcher's mound.

To bunt, get into your batting stance. As the pitcher is about to deliver the ball, turn your body so you are squarely facing the pitcher. Do that by sliding your front foot out a bit and stepping up with your back foot to stand ahead of the plate. As you turn, position the bat to bunt the ball. Keep your bottom hand near the nub but slide your top hand partially down the barrel of the bat. Grip the bat *between* the thumb and fingertips of your top hand. Otherwise, the ball may hit your fingers if you keep them curled around the bat. You would also have less control of the bat.

BUNTING

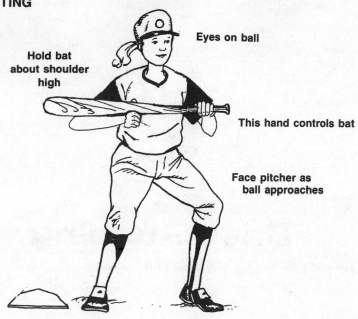

Eyes on ball

Hold bat about shoulder high

This hand controls bat

Face pitcher as ball approaches

Hold the barrel of the bat over the plate in a level position about shoulder high. Assume a slightly crouched position, keeping your head up and your eyes on the ball.

Do not swing at the ball or lunge at it. Let the ball hit the bat as if you are catching the ball. Your hand at the bottom of the bat will help direct where you want the ball to go. Don't move the bat up because any ball higher than your shoulders is not a strike. The only movement of the bat should be down. For a low pitch, bend your knees.

Base Running

Stealing is not allowed in slow-pitch softball. It is allowed in fast-pitch softball after the pitch is thrown. However, neither slow-pitch nor fast-pitch softball allows runners to take leads off bases.

Before you can be on base, you have to reach that base safely. When running to first, run straight down the line and touch the base in stride with your foot. Take a quick glance at where you hit the ball, but do not watch the ball as you run. It will slow you down. Run all the way past the base, making sure you step on it as you go over it. You do not have to stop on first. It also doesn't matter which way you turn after you pass the base. As long as you do not make a move toward second base, you cannot be tagged out.

RUNNING TO FIRST

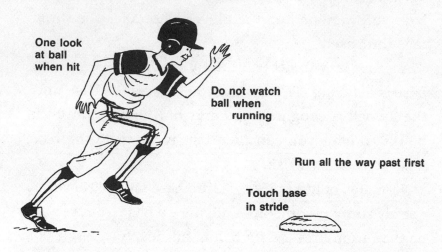

One look
at ball
when hit

Do not watch
ball when
running

Run all the way past first

Touch base
in stride

For extra-base hits, start to turn before you reach the base. Do not run straight to the base and then turn after you pass the base.

Start your turn when you are three to five strides away from the base. It will improve your base-running time. Make sure, however, you touch every base with your foot.

GENERAL RULES

When running bases, you should keep several general rules in mind. One is never pass another base runner in front of you. That base runner will then be out.

Do not run on a fly ball. Slowly head for the next base, then stop partway to see if the ball is caught. If it is caught, go back to the base you came from. If it isn't caught, continue on. If you run on a fly ball that is caught, you can be put out if the ball is thrown to the base you were on and the player who takes the throw tags the base.

Another way to deal with a fly ball while you are on base is to *tag up*. This means you stay on the base until the fly ball is caught. If you stay on the base until the ball is caught, you can then legally move to the next base at your own risk.

Normally, only runners on third base tag up. However, speedy runners sometimes advance a base from second or even from first if a fly ball is hit deeply enough.

TAGGING UP

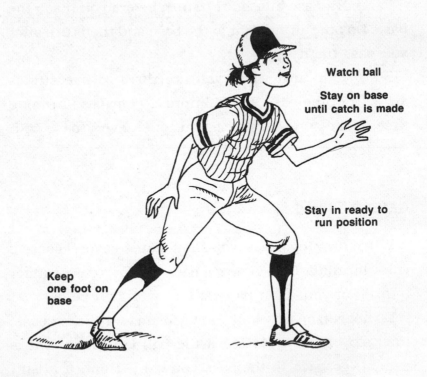

Watch ball

Stay on base
until catch is made

Stay in ready to
run position

Keep
one foot on
base

SLIDING

Sometimes a base runner has to slide into a base to avoid being tagged out. Never slide into first base, however, unless the first-base person is trying to tag you instead of the base.

Sliding is also something that should be practiced only under the watchful eyes of a coach. *Do not* try to teach yourself how to slide.

The straight-in slide is the basic slide beginners should use. Approach the base with your body straight and your eyes on the base. Slide on whichever side of your body is more comfortable for you. It will be explained here on the right side. As you come into the base, bend your right leg at the knee and kick your left leg forward as if you are kicking a soccer ball. Tuck your right leg under your left leg as you throw your hands over your

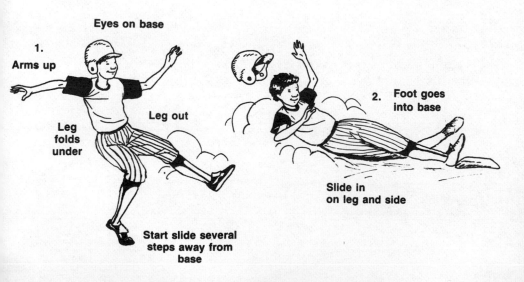

Eyes on base

1.
Arms up

Leg
folds
under

Leg out

Start slide several
steps away from
base

2. Foot goes
into base

Slide in
on leg and side

head and lean back. Get as low as you can. Slide on your hips, not on your knees. Extend your left leg out toward the base. Keep the foot of the bent leg turned sideways.

Now lean your upper body back. Your arms should be up to prevent hand injuries and to keep your body flat. Your hips take the shock of the fall as you slide forward. The extended leg makes contact with the nearest part of the base.

One mistake beginners often make is sliding too late. Always begin to slide when you are three to four steps away from the base.